15 EASY-TO-BUILD
BIRDHOUSES

15 EASY-TO-BUILD
BIRDHOUSES

Simple-to-make birdhouses and bird
tables shown step by step in 120
colour photographs and diagrams

Andrew Newton-Cox and Deena Beverley

LORENZ BOOKS

Dedicated to Jane Wilson

This edition is published by Lorenz Books

Lorenz Books is an imprint of Anness Publishing Ltd
Hermes House, 88–89 Blackfriars Road, London SE1 8HA
tel. 020 7401 2077; fax 020 7633 9499
www.lorenzbooks.com; www.annesspublishing.com

If you like the images in this book and would like to investigate using them for publishing, promotions
or advertising, please visit our website www.practicalpictures.com for more information.

© Anness Publishing Ltd 1997, 2006

UK agent: The Manning Partnership Ltd, 6 The Old Dairy, Melcombe Road, Bath BA2 3LR;
tel. 01225 478444; fax 01225 478440; sales@manning-partnership.co.uk
UK distributor: Grantham Book Services Ltd, Isaac Newton Way, Alma Park Industrial Estate, Grantham,
Lincs NG31 9SD; tel. 01476 541080; fax 01476 541061; orders@gbs.tbs-ltd.co.uk
North American agent/distributor: National Book Network, 4501 Forbes Boulevard, Suite 200, Lanham,
MD 20706; tel. 301 459 3366; fax 301 429 5746; www.nbnbooks.com
Australian agent/distributor: Pan Macmillan Australia, Level 18, St Martins Tower, 31 Market St, Sydney,
NSW 2000; tel. 1300 135 113; fax 1300 135 103; customer.service@macmillan.com.au
New Zealand agent/distributor: David Bateman Ltd, 30 Tarndale Grove, Off Bush Road, Albany, Auckland;
tel. (09) 415 7664; fax (09) 415 8892

A CIP catalogue record is available from the British Library

Publisher: Joanna Lorenz
Senior Editor: Lindsay Porter
Designer: Caroline Reeves
Photographer: David Parmiter
Stylist: Deena Beverley
Illustrators: Lucinda Ganderton and Vana Haggerty

Publisher's Note
*Craft and woodworking projects are very rewarding but when using any tools or equipment, care must be
taken and the proper protective clothing worn as required. The authors and publishers have made every
effort to ensure that all instructions contained within this book are accurate and safe, and cannot accept
liability for any damage or injury.*

Previously published as *Making Birdhouses*

1 3 5 7 9 10 8 6 4 2

Contents

Introduction

Perhaps it is the opportunity to create a world in miniature from almost any material available, while simultaneously giving nature a helping hand, that has ensured the continued popularity of bird-housing as a thriving folk art around the globe.

Birdhouses can be plain, pretty or fanciful without affecting their primary function. Having satisfied the basic dimensional and safety requirements, the finish of the exterior is up to the individual.

The projects in this book are practical and beautiful solutions for providing food, drink and shelter for the feathered community.

Even unoccupied birdhouses make charming decorative features for either interior or garden, and collecting antique birdhouses is a growing trend. We do hope that you take this opportunity to create your own heirloom piece.

From rudimentary woodwork to more complex mixed media creations, there is something here for every level of ability. New skills can be learnt while creating something that will be of lasting benefit and enjoyment to birds and humans alike.

Happy birdhousing.

Providing a Place to Nest

Above: A wicker beehive-style house is ideal for smaller birds, and makes a decorative addition to the garden.

Even in an urban garden, birds will find many nooks and crannies for nesting. Just a little encouragement in the form of providing suitable nesting boxes will ensure that birds breed, as well as feed, in your garden.

Nest boxes

An excellent way to follow birds' progress in your garden is to install a nest box. In addition to the many designs and ideas provided in this book, specialist organizations will give good advice on building rudimentary but effective boxes, together with detailed advice about different species and their preferences.

Choosing a site

There may be natural possibilities already in your garden that, with a little thought, can be turned into good nest sites. Birds may nest in an old shed that has had the door left purposely ajar, or make their homes in a hole in the eaves of a house or outbuilding. Thick hedges, rotten trees, unclipped bramble bushes and log piles are all potential homes. Place any box away from possible disturbances, approximately 2 m (6½ ft) up a wall or tree trunk. Face the box away from prevailing wind and rain, and do not position it to face south, as the sun will overheat the chicks and eggs. Place open-fronted nest boxes in thick cover.

Avoiding predators

Fledglings must learn to survive, so any human intervention is not a good idea, but you can help by attaching a bell to your cat's collar to at least alert birds to the presence of lurking felines. Prickly, cat-deterring plants around the nest sites may help, together with scents to ward off cats, such as proprietary brands and essential oil sprays. The best cat deterrent is probably a dog.

Other threats include magpies, which attack the open-cup nests of birds such as chaffinches and blackbirds. Great spotted woodpeckers, which can hack their way through the side of a nest box, can be put off by adding metal plating to the nest box.

Although it may seem cruel, should you find a fledgling or nestling on the ground, leave well alone and let nature take its course. Remember that nature is about survival of the fittest, and stand clear.

Right: Robins, among other species of bird, enjoy open-fronted boxes.

INSTALLING A NEST BOX

There are a few simple rules to consider when installing a nest box of any type:

• Be patient. It may take several seasons before any birds settle in the boxes. When birds do settle, do not interfere. Enjoy them from a distance.

• Avoid placing a feeding table near to a nesting box. The nesting birds would suffer greatly from the presence of feeding birds so close to their home.

• Be aware that a perch close to the entrance hole may also assist predatory access.

• Be restrained. One or two boxes in the average garden is enough. Any more than that will cause distress.

• Place the nest box in situ in the autumn so that it will weather, and possibly supply winter roosting, for when the spring breeding season arrives.

• Clean out used nest boxes with plain, boiling water at the end of the season (around November) to kill any lurking parasites.

Above: The long chimney-like shape of this box will attract owls, which tend to nest in hollow trees.

Above: Although customized and embellished, this house still retains its practical elements, providing a perch to allow access to the inside and a small entrance hole to keep out larger birds.

Basic types of nest box

There are several types of nest box, each designed for particular types of bird. For example, coal tits need smaller entrance holes than great tits, to prevent the larger bird evicting the smaller one when the almost inevitable territorial disputes arise.

Robins, stock doves, jackdaws, wagtails and spotted flycatchers may make their homes in open-fronted nest boxes. Owls prefer a chimney-like box that mimics the hollow ends of branches they naturally prefer. This type of box is particularly welcome where a known nest site has been lost because of storm damage. Fix the box at a 45-degree angle on a tree, drill drainage holes in the bottom and add a layer of wood chips or stone chippings inside. Owls are protected by law in some countries, and if this is the case, occupied nests should not be visited without a licence – even if you have installed the box yourself. It is a good idea to contact a specialist organization for advice.

Special boxes may also be built for kestrels and woodpeckers. If you are very interested in nature, you will probably want to add homes for hedgehogs and squirrels, too. Specialist organizations are a great source of the latest up-to-date information.

Attracting Birds

Above: Lard cakes studded with seeds appeal to many varieties of bird.

Right: Roofed bird tables will keep the birds - and food - dry in inclement weather. This one was made from pieces of fallen wood collected from the forest floor.

Below: Some source of water should be provided if you are supplying dried foods, particularly in winter.

The simplest way to attract birds to your garden or window box is to put out food for them, particularly during the winter months when natural food becomes scarce. However, you may provide appropriate food throughout the year if you wish.

Whatever feeding method you decide upon, be consistent. A wasted journey to an empty bird table uses a bird's precious energy supply, especially as winter progresses and food becomes more difficult to find. Ideally, feed twice a day in winter: once in the early morning and again in the early afternoon.

In spring and summer, feeding can still be helpful, but do follow these rules for safety and hygiene: do not use peanuts unless they are in a mesh container. This will prevent the larger pieces, which can choke baby birds, from being removed. In summer, avoid fat cakes; the fat will melt and become very messy, and can also glue birds' beaks together.

Above: The wire mesh around the food source keeps birds from extracting whole peanuts. This is particularly important during the nesting season because young nestlings and fledglings can choke on whole nuts.

Where to feed

Ideally, a bird table should be placed approximately 2–3 m (6½–10 ft) from a bush or tree, where the birds can flee in case of danger, and at least 5 m (16½ ft) from a house. Many birds are nervous of open sites, but equally they can have accidents flying into house windows, and may be scared away by the movement of people inside the house. Window stickers featuring birds of prey are available which, when stuck to the window panes, indicate the presence of an otherwise invisible surface and deter smaller birds from flying too close to the house.

Bird tables

A bird table gives you a clear view of feeding birds, and offers the birds some protection against predators and the elements. Use wood that has not been treated with wood preservative if you are making your own table. A roof will keep the food and the birds dry. If you don't make a roof, drill a few holes in the floor of the table for drainage. A small lip around the edge of the food table can prevent lighter food types from being blown away by wind. A bird table must be cleaned from time to time and any food that is past its best should be removed. An adequate supply of water should be provided all year round, which can be as simple as a bowl of water on the surface of the table, or a separate facility.

Below: Seed balls and strings of nuts are a welcome supplement to the meagre diet available in winter. Do keep a supply of fresh water on hand as well, as dried food does not contain enough natural moisture.

Above: Hanging feeders offer an enjoyable challenge to many species.

Feeding from ground stations

Some birds, such as dunnocks and song thrushes, are habitual ground feeders. Pheasants, finches, buntings and turtle doves may also be attracted to ground stations. Place ground stations away from the bird table, if you have one, so that the food is not contaminated by droppings from the birds above.

Hanging feeders

Some species, such as tits, that are adapted to feeding in trees will benefit from a more challenging feeder. Blue and great tits can cling upside-down from various types of hanging feeders, and may be joined by siskins and nuthatches. Many types of feeder are available, or you can make or adapt your own. Some foods are also suitable for hanging without a feeder, such as peanuts in shells, half coconuts, popcorn garlands and fat cakes on strings.

11

What to Feed

Left: A wreath of glazed, sliced cranberries is appreciated by the feathered community.

Live food

Live food, such as waxworms and mealworms, provides a high-quality source of protein and encourages a wide variety of species into the garden. Live food is especially useful during harsh weather and can be obtained from specialist suppliers.

Seeds and grains

Use best-quality seeds from a reliable source, not sweepings or waste seeds as these are neither of interest nor of nutritional value to the birds. Sunflower seeds are a good choice, and black sunflower seeds rather than the striped variety are the favoured food of many species. The skins are the thinnest of all sunflower varieties, making them easy for the birds to open. All types of sunflower seeds are safe for young birds to eat, so they may be offered all year round. Canary seeds, melon seeds, hemp seeds, small wheat, kibbled and flaked maize, corn kernels and oatmeal are all good sources of nutrition. The mix of seeds may be fine-tuned to attract particular species to your garden. Consult a specialist catalogue for more details.

Unsalted peanuts

Buy only high-quality "safe nuts", marked as such by the Bird Food Standards Association or other reputable body, to ensure that the nuts are free from lethal toxins. Ensure that it is difficult to pull a whole, shelled peanut from a feeder, because adult birds have been known to feed these to their young, resulting in fatal choking.

Apart from kitchen scraps, there are many types of food suitable for the birds in your garden. A glance at any specialist catalogue will reveal a mass of foods designed to attract particular birds. Here are just a few ideas.

Fat products

The best types of base for fat cakes are lamb and beef fats, either in natural form or as processed suet. Because these are hard, they do not melt too readily in warm weather, which can potentially glue birds' beaks together. Specialist manufacturers add enticements to their fat cakes but you can easily make your own at home with a mixture of seeds, fruits and nuts following the recipe on the next page.

Bird Treats

SUITABILITY OF GENERAL FOODS

Trial and error will prove what goes down best with your feathered population, but here are a few general pointers:

• *Bread* is eaten by many species. Brown is best, but whatever type you offer, make sure that it has been thoroughly soaked in water to prevent it expanding in the birds' stomachs.
• *Dried fruit* is popular, but should be soaked as for bread.
• *Fresh fruits,* especially pears and apples, are enjoyed by blackcaps and thrushes. It is particularly useful to offer these fruits in winter.
• *Grated cheese* is popular, especially with robins.
• *Grit, sand and gravel,* although not actually foodstuffs, aid digestion, particularly for seed eaters.
• *Hazelnuts* wedged into tree bark will appeal to nuthatches, who will enjoy hammering them open.
• *Household foods* such as hard-boiled eggs, jacket potatoes, uncooked pastry and stale cake and biscuits are all widely available choices that birds will enjoy. Feel free to experiment, taking care not to offer dehydrated or very salty foods, as these can be dangerous.

All of the following recipes are guaranteed to bring flocks of birds to your garden and ensure a happy and satisfied bird population.

Bejewelled apple

An apple stuffed with colourful, nutritious goodies is a visual, as well as a nourishing, feast. Hollow out an apple that is past its best. Fill it with a mixture of cooked rice, seeds, rehydrated dried fruit and berries. Make sure the fruit has been thoroughly rehydrated before mixing.

Berry, seed and golden kernel heart

This delectably pretty treat is very easy to make. In a double boiler, melt down some white fat. Add rehydrated berries, seeds, nuts and corn kernels. Pour into a heart-shaped tin (the size sold for making individual cœur de crème is perfect). Drape a length of natural garden string into the mixture so that it will emerge from the top of the heart for hanging. Weigh the string down with more fruit and nuts if it rises to the surface. Allow to set thoroughly before removing from the tin. Invert the tin and run a little warm water over it to aid release.

Cranberry terrine

This is made in a similar way to the Berry, Seed and Golden Kernel Heart. Place a layer of rehydrated cranberries into the base of an individual oval tin. Slowly pour over just enough melted white fat to secure the berries in place. Leave to cool and set. When set, add more melted fat to form another layer. Allow to cool and set before adding the final layer of berries, secured with a little melted fat. Leave to set, and remove as for the Berry, Seed and Golden Kernel Heart.

Nuts and berries festive loaf

Soak brown breadcrumbs in water until soft. Mix in assorted rehydrated berries, seeds and nuts. Grease an individual loaf tin, and add the mixture, pressing down well. Bake in a moderate oven for approximately 15 minutes or until the top is golden brown and the loaf leaves the sides of the tin. Leave to cool slightly, remove from the tin and cool on a wire rack.

Orange sunrise pudding

Hollow out an orange half, and fill with a mixture of muesli, fruit, nuts and seeds, all fully soaked and rehydrated with water before mixing.

Birdbaths

Above: Running water will appeal to the birds as it enhances your garden.

Above: A traditional stone birdbath is an atmospheric addition to any garden.

Right: This contemporary birdbath is a piece of sculpture in its own right.

Opposite: Pieces of broken crockery make a wonderful mosaic pattern. The sloping sides provide easy access to the water.

Birds need a constant supply of water, for both bathing and drinking. It is essential for them to keep their feathers in good condition for insulation during the long and bitter nights of winter. Some birds, such as blue tits, may drink more in winter because the seasonal diet of dry nuts is not sufficient to hydrate them. Seed eaters also need plenty of drinking water to compensate for the lack of moisture in their diet.

Ponds, of course, provide water all year round for bathing and drinking, and attract many other types of wildlife to your garden. We are not all fortunate enough to have the space or the facilities for ponds or larger water sources, but a birdbath is an attractive option which will brighten your garden while bringing great pleasure to the bird population as well as yourself.

A birdbath need not be an elaborate affair. A puddle is the simplest form of all. You could make a more permanent watering hole by scraping out a shallow puddle shape in a flower bed, lining it with plastic and securing the plastic in place with stones. Another simple and unobtrusive option might be an inverted dustbin lid securely placed on bricks.

There are many commercially available birdbaths which not only serve a useful purpose to the birds, but add points of interest to a garden scheme. Fountains, or any form of dripping water, make ponds and baths even more enticing to birds as well as appealing to human visitors.

Whatever the birdbath, make sure that it has either sloping sides or a ramp if the sides are steep, so that birds can easily walk in and out, and small animals do not become trapped. Do be diligent about keeping the birdbath clean and filled with fresh water, and crack any ice which forms on the surface in the winter.

Daisy House

Summer daisies make a stylish statement for the fashionable nesting pair. Roses or a flower of your choice may be substituted to produce customized garden chic.

● ●

TOOLS AND MATERIALS

- **6 mm (¹/4 in) medium-density fibreboard (MDF) or exterior-grade plywood**
- Pencil
- Ruler
- Saw
- PVA glue
- Hammer
- Panel pins

- Drill
- Padsaw
- Bench vice
- Emulsion paint: white, yellow, green and blue
- Medium and fine paintbrushes
- Glue gun and glue sticks
- Exterior-grade varnish

● ●

1 Mark out the basic house onto 6 mm (¹/4 in) MDF or plywood following the template at the back of the book. Cut out the pieces and assemble with PVA glue and panel pins. Draw flower, petal and leaf shapes onto the face of the board, following the diagram on the next page. Make sure the central hole in the front motif will match the size of the entrance hole.

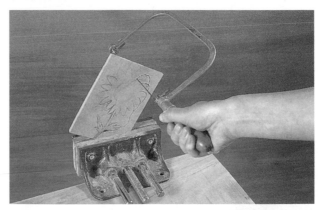

2 Using a coping saw, cut out the leaf and petal shapes. Using a drill and padsaw, cut out the central hole of the front motif. Paint the pieces to represent real daisy colours and leave to dry. Add details with a fine paintbrush. ●●●►

3 Paint the basic house blue. When dry, embellish with painted "grass" applied with a fine paintbrush. Paint the entrance hole with yellow, but leave the interior unpainted for the health of the birds.

Above: If woodworking is not your forte, this simply painted alternative should appeal. The same basic house is painted in bright colours. A slice cut from a cork forms a jaunty perch which mirrors the loosely applied polka dots.

4 Using a glue gun, stick the shapes permanently to the box. Position the shapes to form a "daisy chain" across the box, gluing on some "fallen petals" for added effect. Coat with several layers of exterior-grade varnish.

Rustic Feeders

These two feeders in different styles originate from the same basic shop-bought model. One has been sanded and given a driftwood-style paint effect, while the other has been camouflaged beneath found objects ranging from a rusty tin sheet to plasterer's angle bead. Be free with the choice of found objects you use and give the feeder a flavour of whatever is in its immediate environment, or collect materials while on holiday to produce a delightful memento.

1 Paint the first feeder and allow to dry. Rub down with sandpaper to give the surface a weathered, driftwood effect. Apply clear glue to the roof and sprinkle sand over it. Add seashore finds, such as shells, and moss. Twist lengths of stub wire around a pencil and weave natural twine through them to imitate coils of rope.

TOOLS AND MATERIALS

- 2 wooden bird feeders
- Light grey emulsion paint
- Medium paintbrushes
- Sandpaper
- Clear glue
- Sand
- Shells
- Moss
- Stub wires
- Pencil

- Natural twine
- Corks
- Craft knife or scalpel
- Thick florists' wire
- Protective gloves
- Sheet of old tin
- Tin snips or saw
- Glue gun and glue sticks
- Plasterer's angle bead
- Black spray paint

2 Use cut-off corks to seal the feed chambers, and tie a loop of florists' wire to suspend the house. •••►

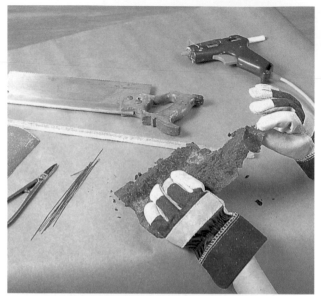

3 For the second feeder, wearing protective gloves, snip pieces of old tin to resemble a roof. Remove all sharp edges and glue in place. Glue moss around the base.

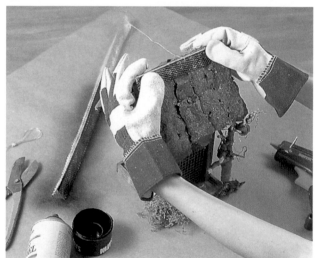

4 Make a ridge for the roof from plasterer's angle bead sprayed black. Glue it firmly to the house. Plug the feed holes with corks and suspend with wire as before.

Above and right: Two very different results are achieved using the same basic feeder. Experiment with different materials and applications to create your own designs.

Beach Huts

*Build multiples of a basic hut and paint them
bright colours to cheer up dull days in the garden.
With separate residences, territorial disputes should
be quickly decided or at least reduced to the simple
question of who gets to live at No. 1, The Promenade.*

TOOLS AND MATERIALS

- 12 mm (¹/₂ in) exterior-grade
  plywood
- Pencil
- Ruler
- Saw
- Pair of compasses
- Drill
- Padsaw
- Hammer
- Panel pins
- 6 x 150 mm (6 in) brass
  hinge strips
- Screwdriver
- Screws
- 6 mm (¹/₄ in)
  exterior-grade plywood
- Coping saw
- Exterior paint: blue, green,
  pink and white
- Medium paintbrushes

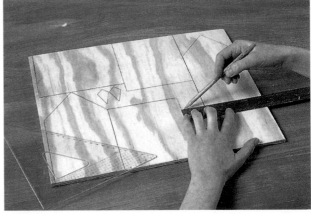

1 Mark the beach hut panels onto the surface of the 12 mm (¹/₂ in) plywood, following the template at the back of the book. You will need to make six basic beach huts.

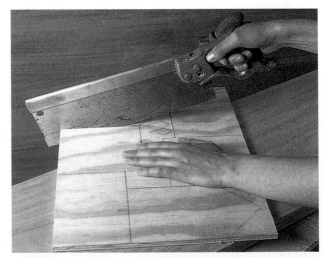

2 Use a saw to cut out each shape. Take care to cut exactly along each pencil line so that the saw cut is divided equally between each panel and the one next to it, to ensure all the pieces are accurate.

22

3 Mark a vertical line on the front panel. Mark a horizontal line across the panel, at the base of the triangle. Where the two lines cross, draw a 32mm (1¹/₄in) circle using a pair of compasses. Cut out the hole by first drilling a pilot hole then enlarging it with a padsaw.

5 Attach the brass hinge strip to the edge of the bigger, loose roof piece using a screwdriver and the appropriate size screws.

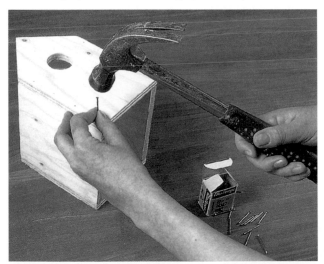

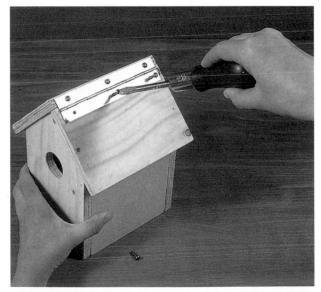

4 Assemble the front, back, sides and the smaller roof piece of the hut using a hammer and panel pins driven flush with the surface of the wood.

6 Attach the hinged roof half to the hut, making sure the two roof halves overlap the front and rear by the same amount.

•••▶

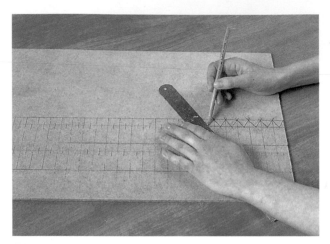

7 Mark out the base and the toothed decorative strips on 6 mm (1/4 in) board. Mark the teeth by drawing a line 20 mm (3/4 in) down from the top edge of each 50 mm (2 in) strip, then ruling off every 20 mm (3/4 in) along the length. Make a pencil mark halfway between each ruled 20 mm (3/4 in) section, then join this single mark with the top line at 20 mm (3/4 in) intervals to form tooth shapes.

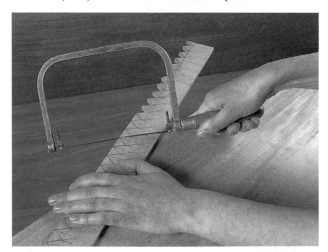

8 Cut the toothing with a coping saw. Fix a toothed decorative strip to each side of the base board with panel pins. Paint as desired with exterior paint, leaving the inside of the huts unpainted for the health of the birds.

Copper Birdbath

You will have endless pleasure watching the birds preening and cleaning in this beautiful yet eminently practical beaten copper birdbath. Maintain a constant supply of fresh drinking water all year round to ensure the health and happiness of the bird population in your locality.

. . . .

TOOLS AND MATERIALS

- Chinagraph pencil
- String
- 0.9mm (20 SWG) copper sheet
- Protective gloves
- Tin snips
- File
- Blanket or carpet square
- Hammer
- Medium copper wire, 4 m (13 ft)
- Bench vice
- Cup hook
- Drill and 3 mm (1/8 in) bit

. . . .

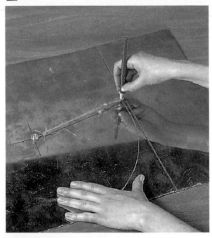

1 Using a chinagraph pencil and a piece of looped string, mark a 45 cm (17³/4 in) circle on the 0.9 mm (20 SWG) copper sheet.

2 Wearing protective gloves, cut out the circle with a pair of tin snips. Carefully smooth any sharp edges using a file.

3 Put the copper on a blanket and hammer it lightly from the centre. Spread the dips out to the rim. Repeat, starting from the centre each time, to get the required shape.

4 To make the perch, loop some copper wire and hold the ends in a vice. Fasten a cup hook into the chuck of a hand drill or slow-speed power drill. Put the cup hook through the loop. Run the drill to twist the wire. Drill three 3 mm (1/8 in) holes around the rim of the bath. Bend a knot into one end of three 1 m (1 yd) lengths of wire. Thread the wires through the holes from beneath the bath. Slip the twisted wire over two of the straight wires to form a perch, and hang in a suitable position.

Miniature Dovecote

Pure folly, this charming miniature dovecote adds a formal note to a sink garden. It is best not left out in the rain, however, so you might prefer to house it permanently in an indoor container or conservatory.

TOOLS AND MATERIALS

• 6 mm (¹/₄ in) balsa wood
• Pencil
• Ruler
• Scalpel or craft knife
• PVA glue
• White acrylic paint
• Medium paintbrushes
• Grey sugar paper
• 6 x 6 mm (¹/₄ x ¹/₄ in) balsa wood stick
• Wood stain

1 Mark the six-sided floors onto the balsa wood, following the template at the back of the book. Cut out using a scalpel or craft knife.

2 Cut the wall panels, angling the long edge cuts so the pieces will fit together neatly.

3 Cut the openings, making several light passes with the scalpel or craft knife rather than a single heavy cut. Cut out the perches.

4 Cut out the roof triangles and glue them together to form a cone. Paint all the parts and leave to dry. Assemble the house using glue. Cover the roof in sugar paper marked with pencil lines to resemble a tiled roof. Cut a stand from a stick of balsa wood, coloured with wood stain.

Dutch Dovecote

This pretty decorative dovecote is just perfect for small gardens and is reminiscent of Victorian gardens of old. You may also find that a few of the local birds like to pay a visit.

TOOLS AND MATERIALS

- 12 mm (¹/₂ in) medium-density fibreboard (MDF) or exterior-grade plywood
- Pencil
- Ruler
- Saw
- Protractor
- Adjustable bevel gauge
- Bench vice
- Plane
- Drill
- Padsaw
- PVA glue
- Wood off-cuts
- Air-dry modelling clay
- Rolling pin
- Table knife
- Cupboard doorknob wrapped in sheet metal or painted grey
- Emulsion paint: white and grey
- Medium paintbrushes
- Exterior-grade varnish

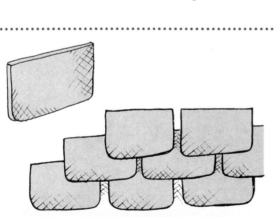

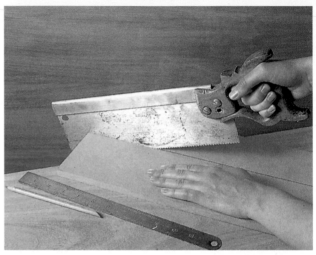

1 Mark the pieces of the dovecote onto MDF or plywood following the template provided. Cut out the pieces with a saw.

2 Use a protractor to set an 18-degree angle on an adjustable bevel gauge.

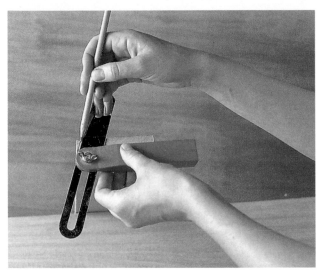

3 Hold the adjustable bevel gauge against each of the ten wood strips and mark the 18-degree angle onto each end with a pencil line.

4 Join the pencil lines along the face of each strip. Carefully run the pencil down evenly along the edge. You may find it easier to use a ruler.

5 Position each strip in a vice and use a plane to remove the waste material down to the marked line. Repeat steps 3–5 for each of the ten roof triangles.

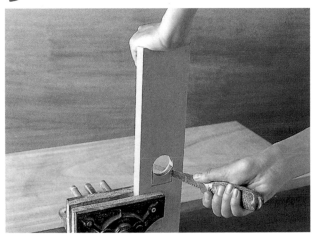

6 Cut ascending entrance holes in five of the ten wall strips, using a drill and a padsaw. Assemble the walls of the house, and glue together along the joints and to the circular base. Cut 6 small wooden blocks from wood off-cuts to use as supports for the removable floors. Fix three at even intervals one-third of the way up the inside of the dovecote, and the remaining three two-thirds of the way up. The dividing floors will simply rest on top of these. Glue the roof triangles to each other but not to the house so the roof and floors are removable for cleaning. Roll out the modelling clay and cut into tile shapes, using the template as a guide. Glue to the roof base, adding the decorated doorknob at the apex as a finial. Paint the body of the house. Varnish the paint and the surface of the roof tiles so the decorative finish will withstand all likely weather conditions.

•••➤

In the nineteenth century, any self-respecting manor house would have had a full-size brick-built dovecote such as this. Sometimes used nowadays as residential buildings or studio workshops, their original function was to keep on hand a supply of fresh meat for lean winter months or an impromptu meal on the arrival of guests at short notice.

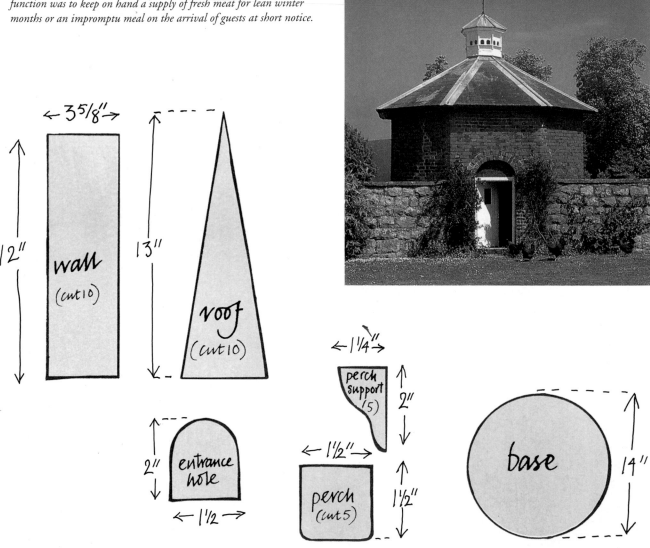

← 3⁵/₈″ →

12″

wall
(cut 10)

13″

roof
(cut 10)

2″ entrance hole

← 1¹/₂ →

← 1¹/₄″ →

perch support (5)

2″

← 1¹/₂″ →

perch (cut 5)

1¹/₂″

base

14″

Clapboard Meeting House

The birds who rear their brood in this New England-style house will be the envy of the neighbourhood.

TOOLS AND MATERIALS

- 6 mm (1/4 in) medium-density fibreboard (MDF) or plywood
- Pencil
- Ruler
- Saw
- PVA glue
- Hammer
- Panel pins
- Birch veneer
- Coloured woodstain
- Scalpel or craft knife
- 1.5 x 19 mm (1/16 x 3/4 in) balsa wood strips
- Pair of compasses
- Emulsion paint: off-white, dark brown and brilliant white
- Medium and fine paintbrushes
- Exterior-grade varnish
- Drill with 3 mm (1/8 in) bit
- 50 x 50 mm (2 x 2 in) wooden post
- Screwdriver
- 75 mm (3 in) screw, plus smaller screws

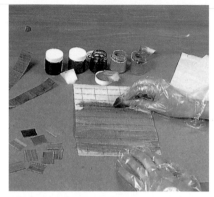

1 Mark the basic house onto MDF or plywood following the template at the back of the book. Cut out the pieces and assemble using PVA glue and panel pins. Mark a sheet of veneer into 19 x 38 mm (3/4 x 1 1/2 in) shingles and rub randomly with woodstain. Cut out the shingles with a scalpel or craft knife. Glue them in overlapping rows to the roof of the house.

2 Cut balsa wood strips to length to use as clapboarding. Glue in position. Set a pair of compasses as a scribe to transfer the cutting angles or make paper templates to indicate the shapes to be cut. Paint the clapboarding with off-white emulsion, and the windows dark brown. Paint on window frames and doors using a fine artist's brush and brilliant white emulsion. Seal the house with exterior-grade varnish.

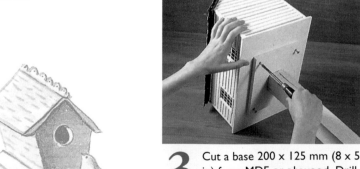

3 Cut a base 200 x 125 mm (8 x 5 in) from MDF or plywood. Drill 3 mm (1/8 in) pilot holes at each corner and in the centre. Fasten to the top of the wooden post with a central 75 mm (3 in) screw. Screw through the corner holes into the base of the house.

Folk-Art Tit Box

This perfect springtime retreat makes an extremely "des res" for blue tits and other hole nesters.

. . . .

TOOLS AND MATERIALS

- 6 mm (1/4 in) medium-density fibreboard (MDF) or exterior-grade plywood
- Small piece of timber *(for base)*
- Pencil
- Ruler
- Saw
- Drill
- Padsaw
- PVA glue
- Hammer
- Panel pins
- Emulsion paint: blue-grey and white
- Medium paintbrush
- Medium-grade sandpaper
- Lead sheet
- Tin snips
- Staple gun and staples
- Copper wire
- Wire cutters

. . . .

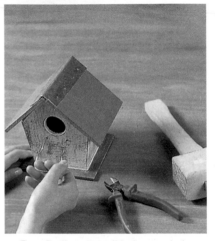

1 Mark the basic house onto MDF or plywood following the template at the back of the book. Cut out the entrance hole as for the Beach Huts. Use PVA glue and panel pins to assemble the basic house. Attach only the shorter roof piece. Paint the whole house, including the loose roof piece, with blue-grey emulsion paint. When dry, paint the walls of the house white. When dry (about 2–3 hours), distress by rubbing with medium-grade sandpaper until a small amount of the darker undercoat shows through randomly. Cut a strip of lead the depth of the roof by 50 mm (2 in) and staple this to the loose roof half. Position the roof halves together, bend the lead to fit and staple through the lead into the fixed roof half.

Right: The tit box can be adapted with different embellishments, and can be fixed on a pole or hung from a tree, as here.

2 Drill two small holes just below and to either side of the entrance hole. Bend a piece of copper wire into a flattened loop slightly wider than the distance between the holes. Pass the two ends of the wire through the holes and turn them down 12 mm (1/2 in) inside the box to hold the perch in place.

Glass Gazebo Feeder

Constructed from recycled tin cans and small pieces of glass, this converted lantern appears jewel-like amongst the foliage.

. . . .

TOOLS AND MATERIALS

- Glass lantern
- Tape measure (optional)
- Thin glass (optional)
- Chinagraph pencil (optional)
- Try-square (optional)
- Glass cutter (optional)
- Ruler
- Protective gloves
- Shiny tin can (not aluminium), washed and dried
- Tin snips
- Flux and soldering iron
- Solder
- Fine wire mesh

. . . .

1 This lantern required extra glass to be installed. If this is the case, measure the areas required and reduce all measurements by 6 mm ($^1/_4$ in) to allow for the metal border around each panel. Using a chinagraph pencil, mark the reduced measurements on the glass, then cut out by running a glass cutter in a single pass along a ruler. Tap along the line to break the glass. It is advisable to wear protective gloves.

2 Wearing protective gloves, and taking care to avoid injury on sharp edges, cut 9 mm ($^3/_8$ in) strips of metal from a used tin can using tin snips. Wrap a strip of metal around each edge of each glass panel. Trim, then smear a small amount of soldering flux onto the mating surfaces of each corner.

3 Solder the corner joints of each panel. Heat up a joint using a soldering iron and apply solder until it flows between the surfaces to be joined. Remove the heat source. The solder will set after 1–2 seconds. Remember that the metal will remain hot for some time after the heat source is removed.

4 Measure the openings for the hoppers and fold sections of metal to suit, using a try-square or ruler to keep the fold lines straight. Solder the meeting points of each hopper. Cut out a platform from fine wire mesh and solder the platform, the panels and the hoppers in place on the gazebo framework.

Hansel and Gretel Cottage

The ultimate in fairy-tale cottage, this two-storey residence with its separate entrances and interior accommodation will brighten up the most sombre garden vista, delighting visiting birds and children alike.

TOOLS AND MATERIALS

- 6 mm (¼ in) medium-density fibreboard (MDF) or exterior-grade plywood
- Ruler
- Try-square
- Pencil
- Saw
- Glue gun and glue sticks
- Scalpel or craft knife
- 6 mm (¼ in) balsa wood
- Emulsion paint: pink, blue, white, dark grey, terracotta, tile red and green
- Medium and fine paintbrushes
- Mounting board
- Drill
- Padsaw
- Acrylic or watercolour paints: various colours
- 1.5 mm (¹⁄₁₆ in) balsa wood
- 1.5 x 3 mm (¹⁄₁₆ x ⅛ in) balsa wood strips
- 100 mm (4 in) hinge strip
- Screwdriver
- Screws
- Double-sided tape
- Scissors
- Fine sawdust
- Exterior-grade varnish

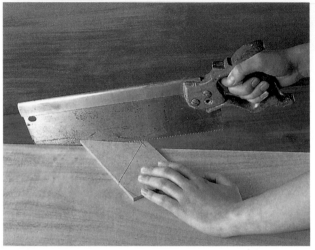

1 Mark and cut out the pieces of MDF or plywood following the template at the back of the book. Assemble pieces 1–8 in order by gluing them together. Cut a "V" in the porch roof as marked on the template.

2 Glue the two roof triangle pieces into the "V" of the porch roof and glue along the ridge.

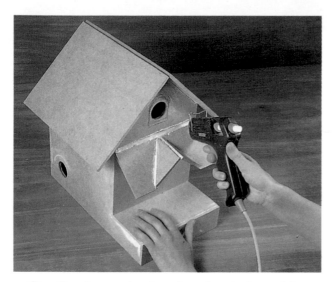

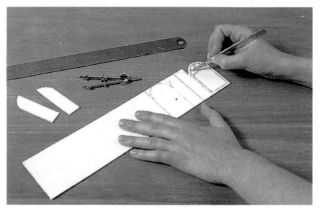

3 Glue the completed porch roof to the front of the house. Using a scalpel or craft knife, cut four 6 x 6 mm ($^1/_4$ x $^1/_4$ in) balsa wood posts, 110 mm (4$^1/_4$ in) long, and glue them in place to support the porch roof. Make sure the posts are upright when viewed from the side as well as from the front. Paint the house with the pink, blue and white emulsion paints.

4 Mark and cut window and door frames from mounting board, following the templates. Use a window frame shape as a template to make shutters. Using first a drill and then a padsaw, cut entrance holes through the house wall where the top front window shape and side door will be. Hold each frame temporarily in position and draw around it with a soft pencil onto the wall. Paint the area within each drawn shape dark grey and leave to dry. Paint "curtains" onto the dark grey with acrylic or watercolour paints. When dry, glue the cut-out window and door frame shapes in place. Decorate the shutter halves with appliqué hearts cut from 1.5 mm ($^1/_{16}$ in) balsa wood and glue on each side of the window frames.

5 Measure from the house walls to the porch corner posts and from the corner posts to the porch centre posts. Cut picket fence posts and top rails from 1.5 x 3 mm ($^1/_{16}$ x $^1/_8$ in) balsa wood and fix in place with glue. •••➤

6 Fit a small dividing wall of MDF or plywood between the main house area and underneath the veranda to prevent young birds from being trapped below.

7 Glue a strip of MDF or plywood halfway up two of the interior walls. Cut the removable dividing floor from MDF or plywood and position it inside the house so that it is supported on the strips when the house is upright. Hinge the house to the base at the bottom of the rear wall, making it possible to raise the house and remove the interior dividing floor for cleaning. Cut out the gable and ridge decoration pieces from 1.5 mm (¹/₁₆ in) balsa wood and glue each in place.

8 Use a scalpel to cut roof tiles 19 x 38 mm (³/₄ x 1¹/₂ in) from mounting board, trimming one end of each tile to form a shallow "V". Lay strips of double-sided tape on a work surface and press the tiles onto the tape. Paint over all the tiles in patches of various shades of terracotta and tile red. Leave until dry. Mark out the roof in horizontal lines 19 mm (³/₄ in) apart and begin tiling, lining up the head of each course of tiles with the pencilled lines. Cut the first tile of each alternate course in half lengthways so that the adjoining tiles will cover the joint line of the tiles in the course below. Complete the painted decoration by touching in any terracotta missing at the roof tile edges and painting on creeper and blossom on the sides of the house. Mix sawdust with green paint to give texture to the "grassy" areas. When all the decoration is dry, give the whole house several coats of weatherproof varnish to finish.

Lavender Hideaway

This hand-painted project takes only a short time to prepare using an inexpensive purchased birdhouse as the basic design. Even the heaviest shower pours freely off the lead roof, leaving the occupants warm and dry within. Take great care when cutting the lead, wearing protective gloves if at all possible.

TOOLS AND MATERIALS

- Wooden birdhouse
- Lilac emulsion paint
- Medium and fine paintbrushes
- Pencil
- Acrylic or watercolour paints: various colours
- Exterior-grade varnish
- Paper for pattern
- Scissors
- Protective gloves
- Thin sheet lead
- Tin snips or craft knife
- Soft hammer or wooden mallet

1 Paint the birdhouse with soft lilac emulsion and allow to dry. Sketch out the decorative design using a pencil. Fill in the sketch using acrylic or watercolour paints. When the paint is dry, cover the whole house with several coats of exterior-grade matt varnish.

2 Make a paper pattern to fit the roof, using the template at the back of the book as a guide. Allow 12 mm (¹/₂ in) extra for turning under each side and the rear, and 32 mm (1¹/₄ in) extra for the scallops.

3 Transfer the design onto a piece of thin sheet lead and cut out using tin snips or a craft knife. Wash your hands thoroughly afterwards.

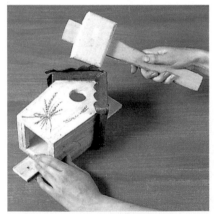

4 Hold the lead roof in place and mould to shape by tapping the lead with a soft hammer or wooden mallet until the correct fit is achieved. Turn the 12 mm (¹/₂ in) allowance under at the back and at the eaves to secure the roof in place.

Log Cabin

This cabin was constructed around a basic box with a sloping roof. One can almost see a wisp of smoke curling from the chimney to welcome a tired spouse home after a long day gathering food for hungry chicks.

TOOLS AND MATERIALS

• 6 mm (¹/₄ in) medium-density fibreboard (MDF) or exterior-grade plywood
• Ruler
• Pencil
• Saw
• Twigs and branches
• Axe or small-scale log splitter
• Glue gun and glue sticks
• Dark grey emulsion paint
• Medium paintbrush
• Drill
• Padsaw
• 100 mm (4 in) x 12 mm (¹/₂ in) coach bolt
• Moss or moss-covered branch

1 Mark the basic house onto MDF or plywood following the template at the back of the book. Cut out the pieces. Make "logs" from small branches by splitting the branches lengthways so there is a flat side for sticking to the box and a rounded surface with bark for the exterior face. Assemble the basic box with a glue gun and paint it with dark grey emulsion paint so that any small gaps between the logs will not show when they are attached.

2 Glue the logs to the front of the house. Cut through the logs into the interior box using a drill and then a padsaw.

3 Cut a 12 mm (¹/₂ in) hole and insert a coach bolt for the "chimney". Continue to fix logs to the rest of the house, shaping them to fit and making the roof logs overlap the walls slightly as an added protection against rainfall. Neaten the corners of the walls by trimming the individual log ends with a saw. Glue a piece of moss or moss-covered branch to the opening as a perch.

Thatched Flint Cottage

The inspiration for this charming cottage comes from traditional thatched roofs.

TOOLS AND MATERIALS

• 6 mm (¼ in) medium-density fibreboard (MDF) or exterior-grade plywood
• Ruler
• Pencil
• Saw
• Glue gun and glue sticks
• Drill and 6 mm (¼ in) bit
• Padsaw
• Double-sided tape
• Exterior-grade filler
• Pea shingle
• Wheat straw
• Thin, malleable wire
• Scalpel or craft knife
• Fine chicken wire
• Emulsion paint: light grey, dark grey and burgundy red
• Medium and fine paintbrushes
• 3 mm (⅛ in) balsa wood
• Exterior-grade varnish

1 Mark and cut out the basic house shapes from MDF or plywood, following the template at the back of the book, and glue together. Cut out an entrance hole, using the drill and padsaw. Cut out window and door shapes from MDF or plywood and temporarily fix them in place with double-sided tape.

2 Apply a thick layer of exterior-grade filler to a small area of the outside of the house. Press pea shingle into the surface of the filler. Continue to apply filler and to press in shingle until the whole house is covered, except for the window and door shapes. Gently remove the temporary window and door "masks" and put to one side for use as templates.

3 Gather together bundles of about 25 wheat straws and tie with thin wire. Glue tied bundles onto the roof of the house until the whole roof is covered. Trim the thatch at the eaves with a scalpel or craft knife and wrap the completed roof with fine chicken wire to secure the thatch.

4 Paint the door and window openings light grey. Paint a lattice of dark grey over the light grey to resemble leaded-light windows. Draw around the window templates onto thin balsa wood and cut out window frames and sills to fit. Make a door from balsa wood and paint it burgundy red. Glue the door and window pieces in place. Paint the base dark grey and coat all exposed wood and paintwork with several layers of varnish.

Rapunzel's Tower

Hidden away in the forest, this romantic tower is truly exclusive. Made from found objects, the final look is dependent on the materials available.

TOOLS AND MATERIALS

- Paper for template
- Pencil
- Garden twine
- Ruler
- Scissors
- 150 mm (6 in) diameter tubing
- 0.9 mm (20 SWG) copper sheet, 450 x 450 mm (18 x 18 in)
- Chinagraph pencil
- Protective gloves
- Tin snips
- File
- Drill and 3 mm ($^1/8$ in) bit and 6 mm ($^1/4$ in) cutter bit
- Blind rivet tool and 3 mm ($^1/8$ in) rivets
- Glue gun and glue sticks
- 0.2 mm (30 SWG) copper foil, 25 x 50 mm (1 x 2 in)
- 65 mm ($2^1/2$ in) nail or wire
- Twigs

1 Make a paper pattern for the cone-shaped roof to fit around the tubing; add a 20 mm ($^3/4$ in) overlap for joining the edges. Transfer the pattern onto a piece of thin copper sheet with a chinagraph pencil. Wearing protective gloves, cut out the shape using tin snips. File off any sharp edges or burrs. Bend the copper into a cone shape with an overlap and check that it fits the tubing correctly. Adjust if necessary.

2 Drill 3 mm ($^1/8$ in) holes at intervals through both layers of copper along the overlap and fasten the overlap using blind rivets. Squeeze the handle of the rivet gun until the rivet shaft snaps off, securing the overlap firmly. Glue the cone in place on top of the tubing.

3 Make a flag for the rooftop by cutting a wavy flag shape from copper foil. Cut a sideways "V" in one end of the flag and bend the other end around a nail or short piece of wire as a flagpole. Glue in place at the tip of the roof.

4 Make a rope ladder by passing cut lengths of small twigs through the weave of two lengths of twine. Cut an entrance hole with tin snips and glue the ladder in place.

Palladian Bird Table

This classical-style feeding table, whether pole-,
tree- or wall-mounted, is simple to make and will
beautify any setting.

· ·

TOOLS AND MATERIALS

- 12 mm (¹/₂ in) medium-density fibreboard (MDF) or exterior-grade plywood *(for the base)*
- 6 mm (¹/₄ in) medium-density fibreboard (MDF) or exterior-grade plywood
- Ruler
- Pencil
- Saw
- Glue gun and glue sticks
- 8 threaded knobs, 30 mm (1¹/₄ in) diameter x 20 mm (³/₄ in) deep
- 4 dowels, 120 x 16 mm (4³/₄ x ⁵/₈ in)
- Drill and 3 mm (¹/₈ in) bit
- Exterior-grade filler
- Fine-grade sandpaper
- Medium paintbrush
- Off-white emulsion paint
- Exterior-grade varnish

· ·

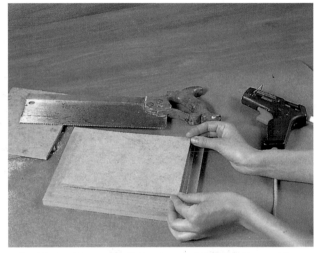

1 Mark and cut out all the pieces, following the template at the back of the book. Assemble the base and steps with hot glue. Mark the positions of the columns at each corner of the top step and on the underside of the ceiling.

2 Glue the main gable triangles onto each end of the ceiling piece.　　· · ·▶

3 Glue each half of the roof onto the top of the gable triangles. Make sure each roof half overlaps the ceiling by the same amount at the sides and each end.

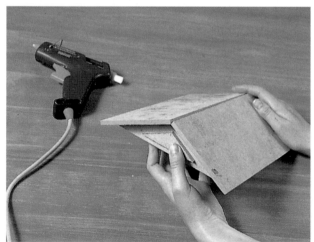

4 Glue the gable decorative triangle centrally onto the face of the front gable.

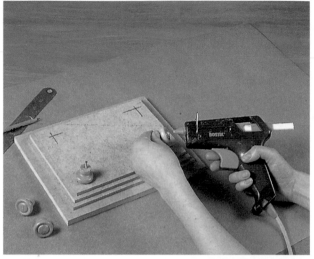

5 Glue the threaded cupboard knobs in position at each corner mark on the base and the ceiling.

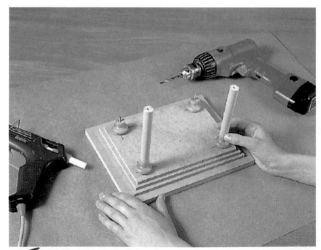

6 Drill each end of the dowel columns to accommodate the protruding thread of the knobs. Apply glue to each thread and assemble the dowels between the base and the roof. Fill any gaps with exterior-grade filler, rub down with fine-grade sandpaper and paint with off-white emulsion followed by several coats of exterior-grade varnish.

Templates

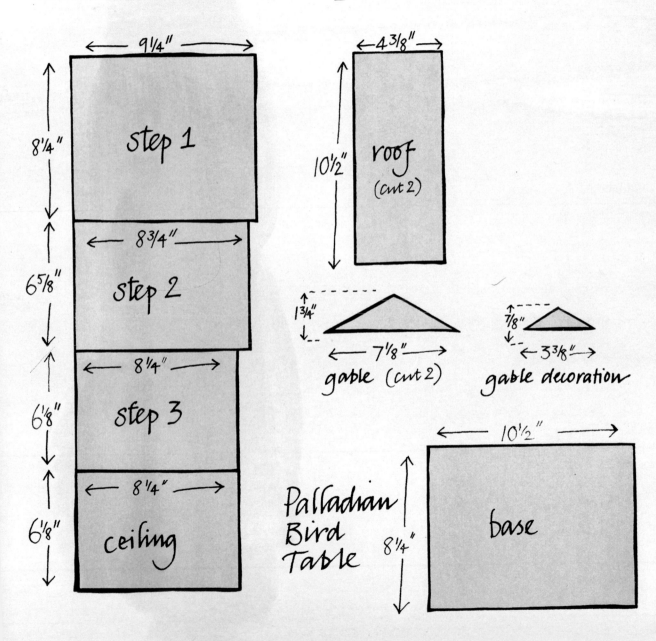

9¼"

step 1

8¼"

8¾"

step 2

6⅝"

8¼"

step 3

6⅛"

8¼"

ceiling

6⅛"

4⅜"

roof

(cut 2)

10½"

1¾"

gable (cut 2)

7⅛"

⅞"

gable decoration

3⅜"

Palladian Bird Table

10½"

base

8¼"

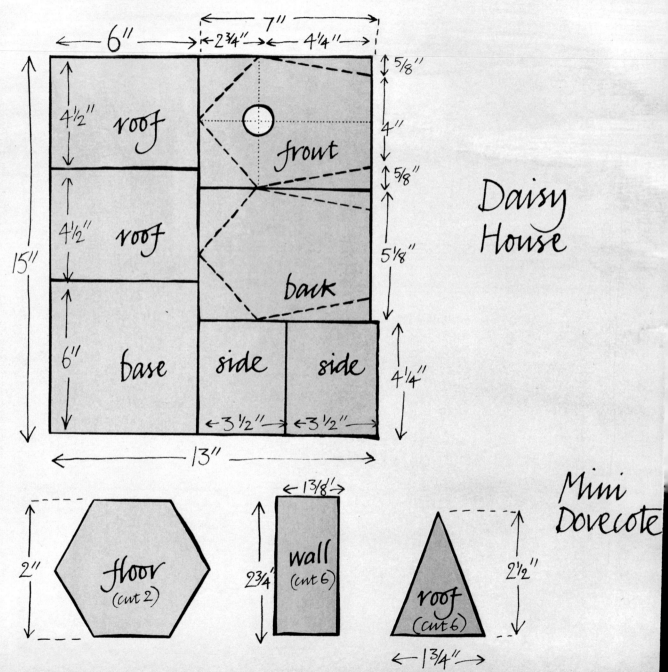

6″

7″

2¾″   4¼″

4½″   roof

15″

4½″   roof

5⁄8″

4″

front

5⁄8″

5⅛″

back

6″   base

4¼″

side   side

3½″   3½″

13″

Daisy House

Mini Dovecote

floor (cut 2)

2″

13⁄8″

wall (cut 6)

2¾″

roof (cut 6)

2½″

1¾″

Beach Huts

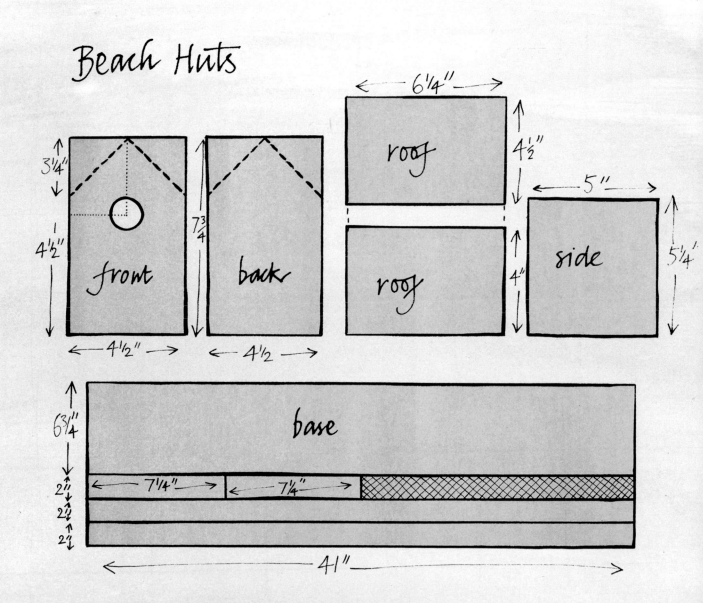

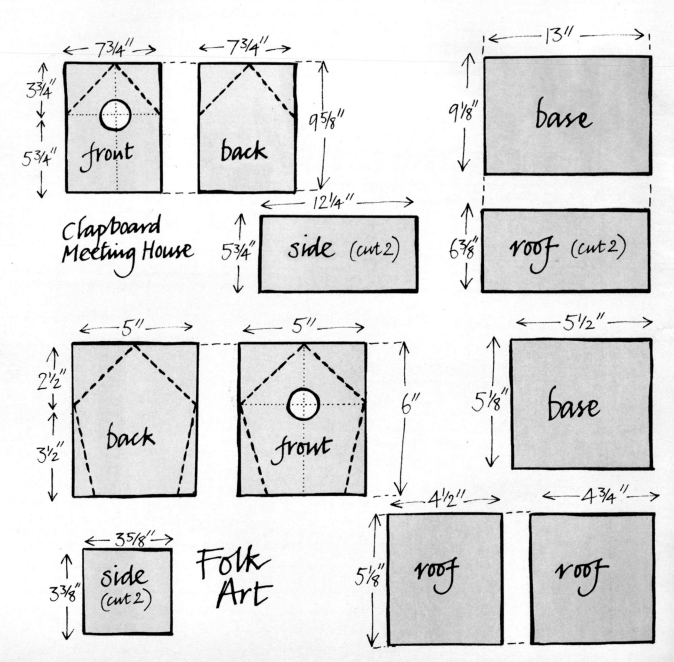

← 7¾″ →

3¾″

5¾″

front

← 7¾″ →

back

9⅝″

Clapboard
Meeting House

← 12¼″ →

5¾″

side (cut 2)

← 13″ →

9⅛″

base

6⅜″

roof (cut 2)

← 5″ →

2½″

3½″

back

← 5″ →

front

6″

← 3⅝″ →

3⅜″

side
(cut 2)

Folk
Art

← 5½″ →

5⅛″

base

← 4½″ →

5⅛″

roof

← 4¾″ →

roof

58

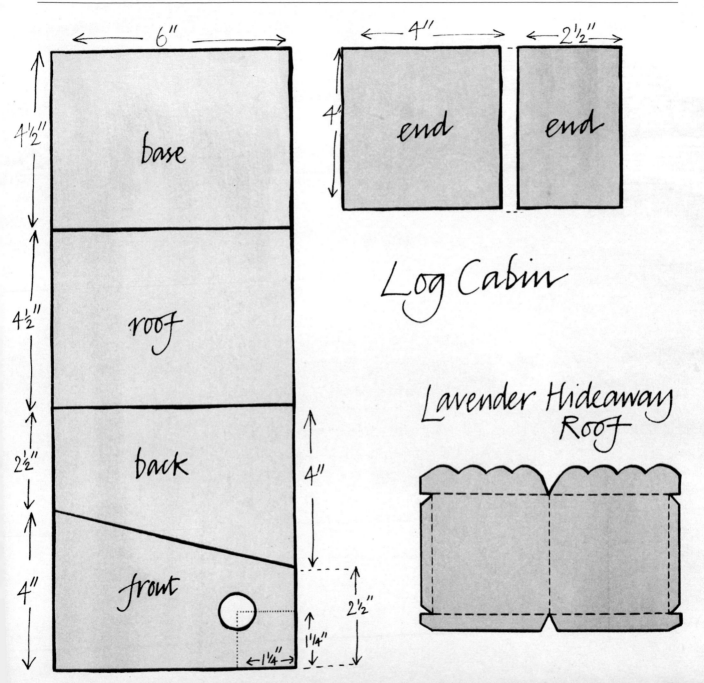

6"

base

4½"

4½"

roof

back

4"

2½"

front

4"

1¼"

1'4"

2½"

4"

4"

2½"

end

end

Log Cabin

Lavender Hideaway
Roof

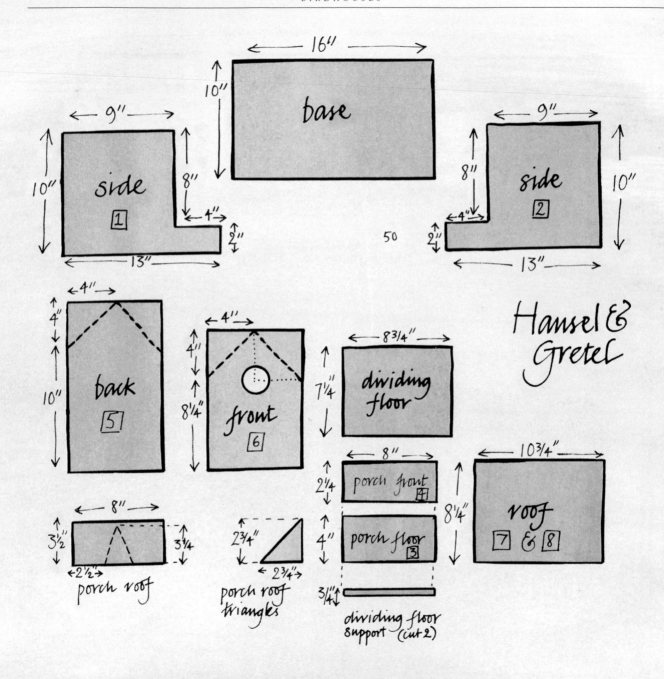

16"

base

9"

10"

side
1

8"

4"

2"

13"

9"

side
2

8"

4"

2"

10"

13"

50

4"

4"

back
5

10"

4"

4"

front
6

8¼"

8¾"

dividing
floor

7¼"

Hansel & Gretel

8"

porch front
4

2¼"

10¾"

roof

7 & 8

8¼"

8"

porch floor
3

4"

3½"

8"

3¾"

2½"

porch roof

2¾"

2¾"

porch roof
triangles

3¼"

dividing floor
support (cut 2)

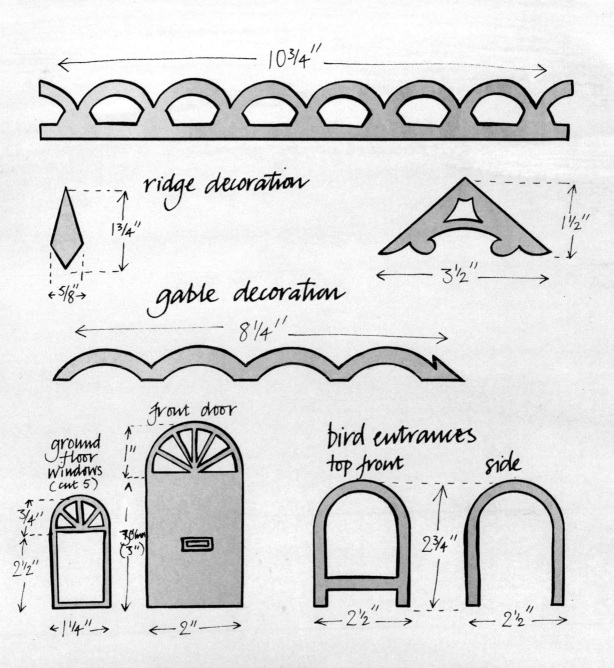

10¾″

ridge decoration

1¾″

⅝″

1½″

3½″

gable decoration

8¼″

front door

ground floor windows (cut 5)

bird entrances
top front   side

1″

¾″

2½″

76mm (3″)

2¾″

1¼″   2″   2½″   2½″

61

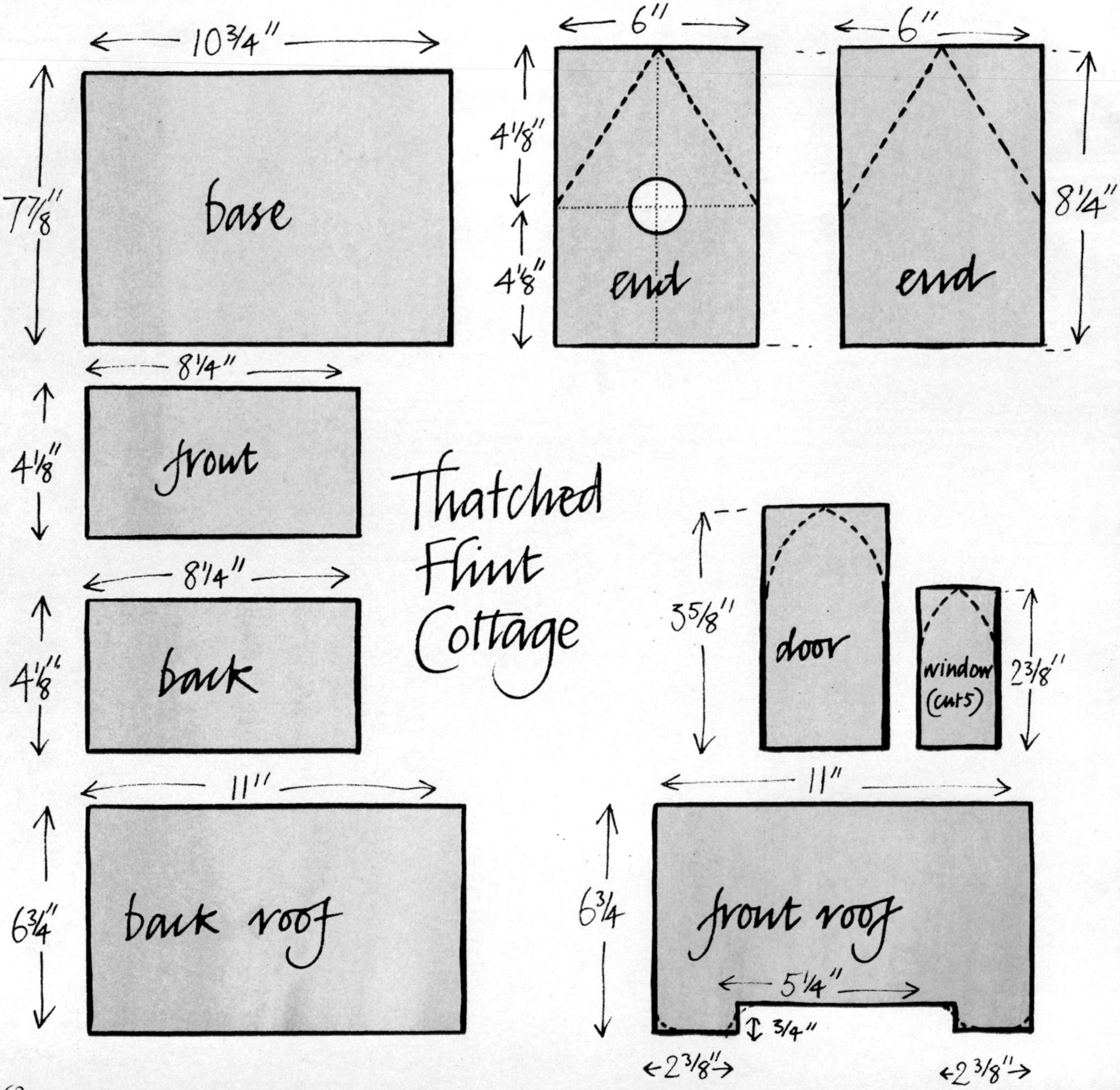
10¾″
7⅞″
base
6″
4⅛″
4⅛″
end
6″
8¼″
end
8¼″
4⅛″
front
Thatched
Flint
Cottage
8¼″
4⅛″
back
3⅝″
door
window
(cut 5)
2⅜″
11″
6¾″
back roof
11″
6¾
front roof
5¼″
¾″
2⅜″
2⅜″

Further Information

WILDLIFE ORGANIZATIONS

United Kingdom

British Trust for Ornithology
National Centre for Ornithology, The
Nunnery, Thetford, Norfolk IP24 2PU
tel: (01767) 680551

Royal Society for the Protection of Birds
(part of the worldwide organization,
Birdlife International)
The Lodge, Sandy, Bedfordshire
MK19 2DI
tel: (011842) 750050

Australia

Royal Society for the Prevention of
Cruelty to Animals
See your local telephone directory for
the branch nearest you.

STOCKISTS AND SUPPLIERS

United Kingdom

Fred Aldous
37 Lever Street, Manchester M60 1UX
tel: (0161) 236 2477
(Sheet metal by post)

C J Wildbird Foods Ltd
The Rea, Upton Magna, Shrewsbury
SY4 4UB
tel: (01743) 709545
(Specialist bird seeds, foods etc)

Forsham Cottage Arks
Goreside Farm, Great Chart, Ashford,
Kent TN26 1JU
tel: (01233) 820229
(Dovecotes)

Carlo Jolly
Hammer Farm, Haselmere
Surrey, GU27 3DE
tel: (01428) 643767

Stilmore Homes
28 Hilliats Field, Drayton, Nr Abingdon,
Oxon OX14 4JQ
tel: (01235) 534902
(Miniature dovecotes)

Australia

Paint-N-Time, Shop 3a, 2–4 Campbell
Street, Northmead, NSW 2152
tel: (02) 630 3775
(Ready-made birdhouses, plus craft and
painting workshops)

Timber Turn
1–3 Shepley Avenue, Panorama SA 5041
tel: (08) 277 5540
(Ready-made birdhouses in a variety of
styles and shapes)

FURTHER READING

The Birdfeeder Handbook, Robert Burton,
RSPB/Dorling Kindersley
Birdhouses, Peri Wolfman and Charles
Gold, Clarkson Potter, 1993
Birds in Your Garden, Nigel Wood,
Hamlyn, 1985

PICTURE CREDITS

Michelle Garrett: p11 bottom; Habitat:
p8 top; Debbie Patterson: p14, p15
(Designer: Cleo Mussi); Spike Powell: p2;
Wildbird Foods Ltd: p11 top left and
top right.

AUTHORS' ACKNOWLEDGEMENTS

*We would like to thank the following people
who contributed so much to this project in
terms of support, advice and locations for
photography:*

Dominique Coughlin, for putting us in
touch with Carlo Jolly, who supplied the
Beach Huts.
Dave Chitson, of Stilmore Homes, for
the Miniature Dovecote.
Forsham Cottage Arks for the loan of
the wall-mounted dovecote, shelf and
terracotta feeders and pots.

Thanks to Bostik for supplying glues and
glue guns; 3M for spray adhesives;
Crown Paints for paint products and
Bosch for power tools.

Thanks to Chris and Pat Cutforth for
their stunning locations and
ornithological advice, and Robin Nelson
and the R.S.P.B. for advice on birds.

Thanks to the National Trust for
permitting photography at Avebury
Manor, and to Dr and Mrs Cameron for
permission to photograph their barn and
dovecote.

63

Index